# Contents

Nelson

# My baby

He's a very shy baby,
my baby.

Holds his hands up high baby,
reaching for the sky baby,
my baby.

Spits out his pie baby,
won't even try baby,
can't tell you why baby,
my baby.

Loves to wave goodbye baby,
kisses you when you cry baby,
wouldn't hurt a fly baby,
pokes you in the eye baby,
my baby!

Living in a noisy household –
with four children and assorted
pets – I tend to see the funny
side of things.  Most of these
poems arose from something I
heard in the garden or the
kitchen, or coming from the den
someone made under the bed.
Perhaps they'll make you think
of things you've said or done.
Poems don't have to rhyme but I
like ones that do.  I sometimes
like them to end in a way you're
not expecting, too!

# Yuck!

Jam all over her fingers,
pastry in her hair,
fruit juice dribbling down her chin
and custard everywhere.

Playdough in her fingernails,
mud between her toes,
and something much, much nastier
running from her nose.

But none of that would bother me,
if it weren't for this:
my sister's heading this way fast
and it's *me* she wants to kiss!

# Chickenpox

"What's it like with chickenpox?"
my little sister said.
"Will you get better? Does it hurt?
I wish *I* were in bed."

"You're lucky, lying here all day,
just listening to tapes.
Your face looks horrid. Does it itch?
Who gave you all those grapes?"

"You *choose* your lunch. I have to have
whatever Mummy eats.
It isn't fair. I'm *never* ill.
You get *all* the treats!"

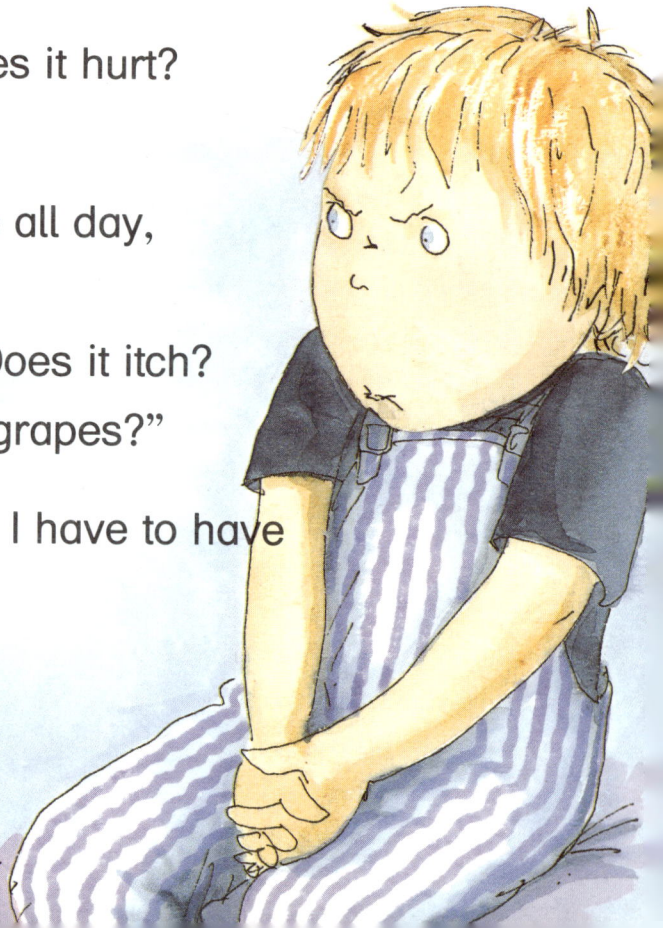

# Little sister

To have a little sister,
you need to be a saint.
You get the pencils out for her,
and then she wants to paint.

You get the paintbox out for her,
and then she wants to play.
You go and get her *all* her toys,
and then she walks away!

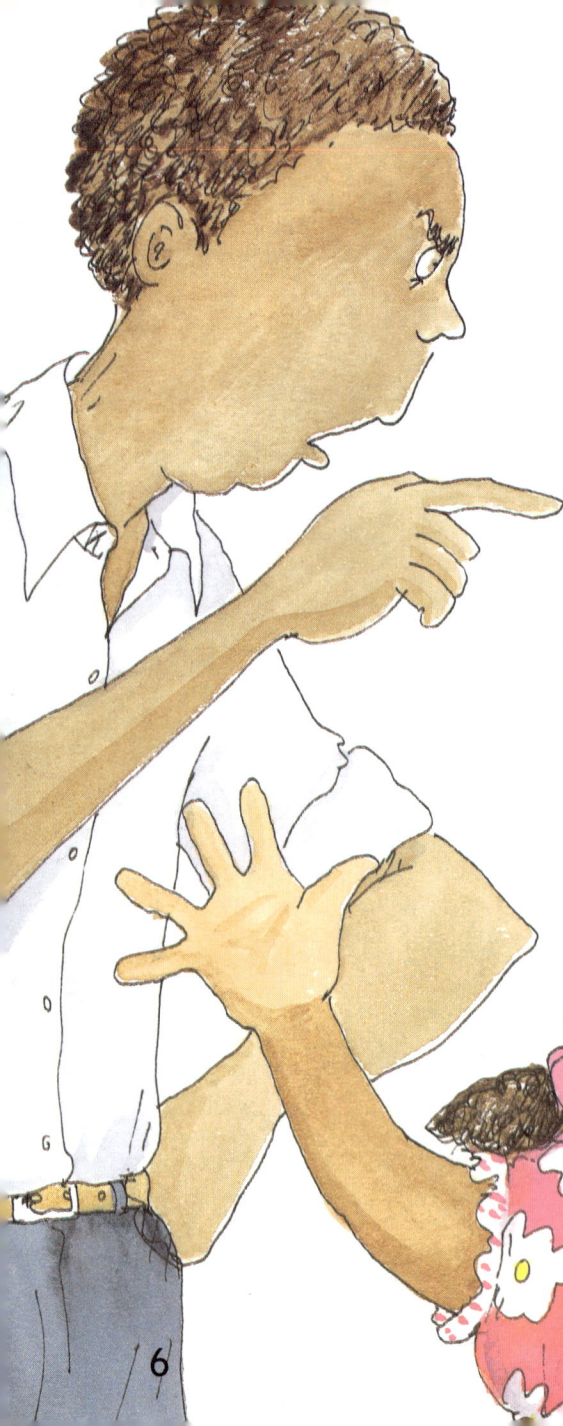

She never stops reciting
the same old nursery rhymes.
I must have heard her favourite one
a hundred million times.

You give up doing what you want
to go and play her game.
Then when she starts to scream and shout,
it's you that gets the blame!

In grown-up games, to help her out,
you give her heaps of clues.
Once I used to cheat to win.
Now I cheat to lose!

You sit there in the Wendy house,
pretending she's your wife.
You end up doing *anything*
to have a quiet life.

# Sick

We're full of bones, my brother says,
inside this bag of skin.
We'd rattle if it weren't for all
those squidgy bits stuffed in.

But even worse, my brother says,
(I'll get this over quick):
all our lives we walk around
with tummies full of sick!

# Can you guess?

Is he brave? You must be joking!
Is he kind? Don't make me laugh!
Is he rough, unfair, a bully,
vicious, spiteful, mean? Not half!

Is she kind and gentle? Never!
Sweet? She couldn't ever be!
Is she bossy, vain, big-headed,
jealous, sly? You're telling me!

Does he love her, though? I think so.
Is he fun? Well, sometimes, yes.
Are they neighbours? Playmates? Cousins?
No. What are they? Can you guess?

# Not funny

My brother's cruel to insects.
I won't say what he does.
But when he's finished with a fly,
it doesn't want to buzz.

A scrabbling spider makes him laugh,
trapped inside a cup.
You find them still inside next day,
completely frazzled up.

As for daddy-longlegs,
he doesn't think they mind.
"They get away -  what if they leave
a leg or two behind?"

I tell him it's not funny.
"What if *you* lost an arm?
They're living creatures, just like you.
It's wrong to wish them harm."

*If I were a giant,*
*I'd trap him like a fly,*
*and pull off all his arms and legs*
*and leave him there to cry!*

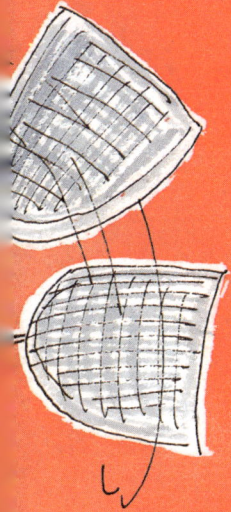

# Dare

My brother ate a tadpole.
*I* dared him, I admit.
But when I did, I never thought
he'd really swallow it!

He says he didn't bite it.
I wonder if it's died.
It could be wriggling round right now,
deep in his inside.

What if it turns into a frog,
and tries to hop away?
Thank goodness he refused to drink
that frogspawn yesterday!

# Friends again

My brother bashed me with a stick.

I hit him with the hose.

He pulled my hair. I scratched his face.

He thumped me on the nose.

I bit his leg. He screamed. I screamed.

We called each other names.

Then Mum came out and asked us why

we couldn't play nice games.

I sulked. He moped. I frowned. He smiled.

I let him in my den.

He offered me a sticky sweet.

And now we're friends again.

# Not for girls

"This game is not for girls," he said,
and crawled inside the tent.
I cried a bit. That didn't work.
So in the end I went.

I got out all the pots and pans,
every single one.
I banged till I felt better,
then I banged some more for fun.

"What are you doing there?" he said,
"Making all that noise!"
"Shut up!" I told him. "Go away!
This game is not for boys."

# You're it

You're it!
Den's the tree,
Who's playing?
*Not me!*

Let's play
ball instead.
You're in goal.
*Who said?*

Either you play,
or I quit.
What do you say?
*I'm it!*

# A great discovery

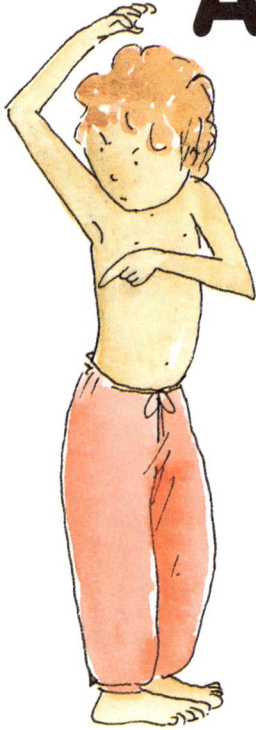

I've made a great discovery,
proved beyond all doubt.
What I did to prove it
nearly wore me out.

Sides and armpits, knees and feet -
I tried it everywhere.
Standing, sitting, lying down;
I tried it dressed *and* bare.

I tried it every way I could.
That's how I know it's true.
And just to check, I went and asked
my friends to try it too.

It can't be done -  it really can't.
All of them agree.
I'm ready now to tell the world
my great discovery:
*You cannot tickle yourself.*

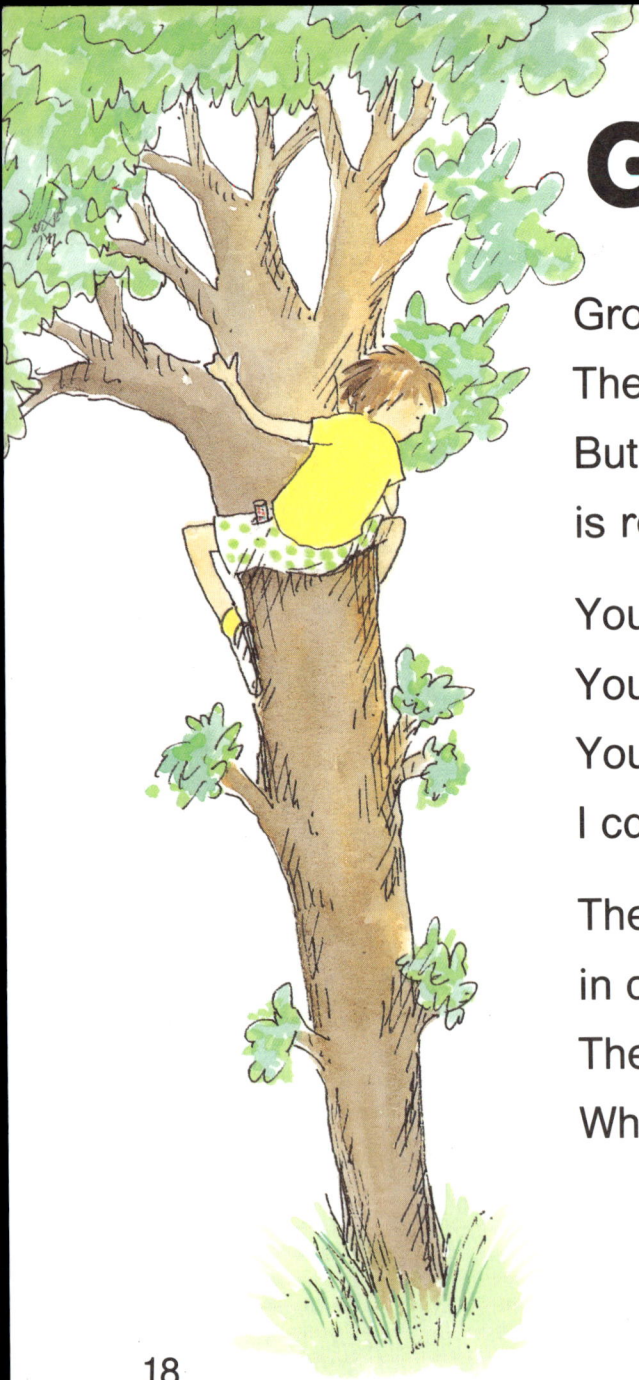

# Grown-ups

Grown-ups *can* be useful.
They help you if you're stuck.
But growing up, if you ask me,
is really rotten luck.

You can't be naughty for a start.
You're not supposed to cry.
You have to act dead sensible -
I can't imagine why.

They don't climb trees; they don't eat sweets,
in case they get too fat.
They just sit round and talk. I *ask* you:
What's the fun in that?

Of course I know it's not all bad.
Some of it's all right,
like driving cars and being tall
and staying up at night.

But don't they understand it's *fun*
to slide down muddy banks?
All they seem to care about
is saying "please" and "thanks".

I know I've got to grow up too.
(I'm not sure how or when.)
It can't be helped. But you can bet
I'll have some fun till then!

# Harriet's dad

Melanie's dad wears an overall.
Philippa's dad wears suits.
But Harriet's dad wears a big glass hat,
and giant-sized wellington boots.

Melanie's dad goes to work on his bike,
and sometimes has oil on his face.
Philippa's dad has an office in town,
with a personal parking place.
But Harriet's dad is an astronaut,
and goes to work in space.

Melanie's dad is always around.

He meets her from school each day.

Philippa's dad gets home too late,

but came to the Christmas play.

But whenever there's anything on at school,

Harriet's dad's away.

# Stagefright

Tonight's the first performance
of our school Christmas show.
Mum and Dad and Grandma
are in the second row.

I peeped out through the curtains,
and saw them coming in.
What's going to be the hardest thing
is trying not to grin.

I come on in the crowd scenes.
I'm second from the right.
And if I stand on tiptoe,
they'll see me - well, they might.

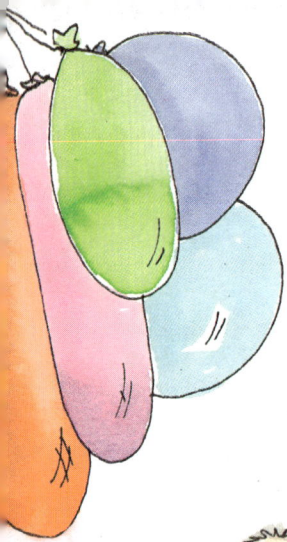

I have to look all puzzled,
but I'm not allowed to frown;
if I do, what happens is,
my helmet slips right down.

It's not a very big part.
I don't have much to say.
In fact I only have two words,
and those are both "Hooray".

But everybody's watching -
all thirteen squashed up rows.
And there's my cue! The moment's come!
Deep breath, chin up - here goes!

# Sulks

Don't talk to me. I'm sulking.
I want to be alone.
How can I sulk properly
unless I'm on my own?

*You* wouldn't feel like eating
if *you'd* just lost your purse.
And trying to be all friendly
will only make it worse!

I want to feel as miserable
as anyone can be.
And when I've felt it long enough –
I'll come downstairs for tea.